THE END OF MICHELANGELO

BOOKS BY DAN GERBER

POETRY

The End of Michelangelo

Particles: New and Selected Poems

Sailing through Cassiopeia

A Primer on Parallel Lives

Trying to Catch the Horses

A Last Bridge Home: New and Selected Poems

Snow on the Backs of Animals

The Chinese Poems

Departure

The Revenant

NOVELS

A Voice from the River

Out of Control

American Atlas

SHORT STORIES

Grass Fires

NONFICTION

A Second Life: A Collected Nonfiction

Indy: The World's Fastest Carnival Ride

The End of Michelangelo

Dan Gerber

COPPER CANYON PRESS

PORT TOWNSEND, WASHINGTON

Cover art: Dan Gerber

Copper Canyon Press is in residence at Fort Worden State Park in Port Townsend, Washington, under the auspices of Centrum. Centrum is a gathering place for artists and creative thinkers from around the world, students of all ages and backgrounds, and audiences seeking extraordinary cultural enrichment.

Library of Congress Cataloging-in-Publication Data
Names: Gerber, Dan, 1940– author.
Title: The end of Michelangelo / Dan Gerber.
Description: Port Townsend, Washington : Copper Canyon Press, 2022. |
    Summary: "A collection of poems by Dan Gerber"-- Provided by
    publisher.
Identifiers: LCCN 2022017859 (print) | LCCN 2022017860 (ebook) |
ISBN 9781556596599 (paperback) | ISBN 9781619322646 (epub)
Classification: LCC PS3557.E66 E53 2022 (print) |
LCC PS3557.E66 (ebook)
    | DDC 811/.54—dc23/eng/20220511
LC record available at https://lccn.loc.gov/2022017859
LC ebook record available at https://lccn.loc.gov/2022017860

9 8 7 6 5 4 3 2 First Printing

Copper Canyon Press
Post Office Box 271
Port Townsend, Washington 98368
www.coppercanyonpress.org

For Peter Phinny
1949–2021
in Loving Memory

Animals trusted him, stepped
into his open look grazing.
And how often the landscape,
overburdened by day,
came to rest in his silent awareness, at nightfall.
RAINER MARIA RILKE

Acknowledgments

Once again, I want to thank everyone who helped bring this book into being: Michael Wiegers, editor, publisher, and friend, for his encouragement and attention to my poems; Copper Canyon Press copublishers Joseph Bednarik and George Knotek; managing editor John Pierce; staff members Janeen Armstrong, Elaina Ellis, Claretta Holsey, Marisa Vito, and Ryo Yamaguchi; David Caligiuri and Alison Lockhart, the most consummate of proofreaders; and Gopa Campbell for the book's exquisite design. Thanks also to friends whose suggestions made some of these poems better—and better together— including Ted Kooser, Joseph Stroud, and Jane Hirshfield. Thanks most especially to Robert Wrigley for his close reading of the original manuscript and his generous advice on its arrangement, and to Kim Barnes for her gift of the book's title. Special thanks to Peg Quinn for reading a number of these poems and for sending a poem by Masahide that prompted the "unpoemed title" regarding the moon in my barn. Finally and foremost, my love and gratitude to Debbie Gerber for keeping me well fed, cared for, and feeling loved through the long pandemic, during which most of these poems were written. I also want to thank the editors of the journals—*The Café Review, Caliban, The Dunes Review, Narrative, Poetry East, Rattle, The Sun,* and *3rd Wednesday*—in which some of these poems originally appeared; Jerry Reddan, whose Tangram Press produced fine broadsides of several of these poems; and Nick Baute at Hound Dog Press and designer Jonathan Greene for the chapbook they produced of "Landscape at Eighty."

Contents

II

III

THE END OF MICHELANGELO

I

*Consciousness seems like a mirror of water which shows
the viewer now the sky, now the depths; and often the water
is jostled and stirred, and makes a multitude of mirrors
and transparencies, an inextricable image.*

PAUL VALÉRY

Walking toward the End

I'm beating north again,
a thousand miles

from the pole, and as it's
still late summer, I

may get a long way
before cold nights

and the hunger of old age
consume me, a little

lighter each day, having
left more of life's

sweet confusion in
the grasses I've been

tracking through since
crossing above

the tree line a week ago,
toward something

I sense I've always been,
my hunger and discomfort only

physical, slaked by the joy

of having nothing
but the next low ridge ahead,

as far as I can see.

World

There is nothing in the picture
you don't see. That is, there

is nothing in the picture, but
you can't see it, as there

is also nothing beyond the picture,
which you can see. As you watch

the picture and begin to notice
more, the nothing grows less, but

never less than nothing. For you,
the picture has no separate

being, and, like you, the
nothing in the picture exists.

As children, we learn to see a ball, a tree,
a dog sitting at the moment.

The dog knows little of our confusion, and
yet calms us with her eyes.

Staying Home

for Deb

It felt like hiding out, you said,
waiting for the plague to die down,

keeping watch for the lives left behind.
You said you saw a soaring hawk let go

a great white glittering shit,
a handful of tinsel in the wind,

making the sky even more blue.
I saw it too from the other side

of the house where I'd been alone,
bowing to the landscape for absorbing me

all afternoon, as I sat there. I don't know
where the time went while I was waiting,

as if for a sign, to come find you.

Practice

Seeing his bodily form, alive
in the grass and trees,

becoming a small stone, tumbling
through a clear stream,

stretching out the space
between two thoughts

waiting around a silence in which
the thought can still hear him breathing.

In Praise of Blue

The brain has never seen the sky, but
through the eye's translation

enjoys the colors it receives, and then,
there's blue, the presence

of the light of which, we know,
even the sightless can sense,

a light within? a color
into which we're born, or

borne out of, on a whim?
color of grieving in ancient Rome, of

ecstasy in Greece, of divinity
in Egypt, of Renaissance virgins, lavished

in ultramarine, of infinite
distance, of mourning dove's moan;

lying awake in bed, deciding,
if only to delight

in blue, as I perceive it, to be
alive another day.

Friday

I got an all clear on the
biopsy of a false-positive that kept

my life dancing, for a week, near the
edge of a cliff, trying to meditate in

a quiet room with one fat fly
waking up to buzz every fifty-

seven minutes, to remind me
he is there.

Mono no aware

I don't know just when it
caught up to be with me. Maybe

it had been gathering, always, like
dust and only now accruing enough

weight to become a presence, as
if the experience of my lifetime

had been harnessed as a team
alongside my present, every step,

playing to the moment of my being
like a lenticular cloud or a nugget

of clear amber, some beacon of delight
within the sadness of things, a silent,

second actor in
every closely watched scene.

Blue Oak

The leaves, a sort of wavy egg-
shape, not yet quite settled on,

bear no blue unless
you see them against the darker

green of the live oaks, or perhaps
in the vast field of the sky from which

they borrow a saturation
of blue, attuned now to

see a green less green, a pale, faded,
dust, or is it frost? a green

somehow kind of blue, you guess,
you don't know what to call its

lusterless look and so
accept, as the book says, "Blue."

Earth Baby

From the scattering of what, at first, appear
to be the body parts of scorpions, he

tries to imagine the chaos, the
arcs and thrashing in the absolute

dark, the squeaks and wash
of wings and teeth from above.

He thinks he's found one still
alive on a flagstone

step, its black-and-tan, segmented
carapace stirring a moment,

and then again. But when
he crouches down close, it's only

the jostle of scavenging
bees, humming inside the now scoured-

out and nearly luminous shell of
the dark Jerusalem cricket, not

a cricket at all, or even
a true bug, perhaps the most

grotesque appearance of God's
natural children, its outsized,

anthropomorphic head, summoned
from dark soil—*bald-headed man*

to the Navajo, *niño de la tierra*
to the Spanish—cleaning up

rotten roots, aerating soil,
perishing in sunlight, they

emerge as a nightly sacrifice to the
eave-hanging bats of his house, bats

rapt in the sonar of their desire and
giddy, in terror of the owl.

Aerial

How soon again after the rain,
finespun streaks of sunlight appear

shooting up filaments a marauding
spider has left in its wake,

flash of meteor tracks
in the moving air, against the

umber backdrop of the oaks, tracing
each pendulous swing to the next

eave-gutter or branch,
only to step out again on the

back of another available breeze,
riding its capricious arc

of arrival to the
surprise of its own design.

Endurance

For a minute or more,
I watched the little brown moth—

no bigger than a nickel—
batter the nap of its wings

ragged against the silvery wings
of the anti-moth, countering

its every stroke in the dark pane
of the window it struggled to climb

and fell back from—watched it
flay its wild life

against the adamant glass
until it felt cruel and I

wondered if my
watching weighed it down.

Exposure

A huntsman spider
in the Namib Desert
emerges from her den
and freezes,
absorbing a pattern of light
from low-hanging stars along
an empty horizon.

She forms an internal map by which
to find a mate on the featureless sands,
her many arachnid eyes drinking
in sidereal light, as

the Hubble locks its shutter open
to the darkest regions of space, until
the infinite, with infinite patience, relents
to reveal the splendor
of a thousand new galaxies tonight.

Butterflies

Like the wings of butterflies
that couldn't fly, Neruda wrote

of poppies as he
saw them as a child, as I

saw them in the meadow
above the house, something

bright orange and moving
in the breeze against a field

of starry filaree, for a
moment not subtracted

from my life, half
expecting them to rise

in search of other flowers.

Crow

I adore the showy non-
chalance of the crow dropping

down to the sidewalk out
of the oak, simply

stepping off his high perch
into the empty air, as if

into a desired oblivion, a
fragment of night, falling

straight down, dead-still;
flaring his wings—almost

an afterthought—an
instant above the terminal

concrete, just now
remembering, again, to survive.

Fly Away Home

On the mountain above us, I
find a billion ladybugs one

winter day on a lightly forested
south-facing slope with sapling pines

sagging under the weight of perhaps
several hundred insects encrusting a single,

willowy limb, the kinetic orange ground
around them teeming, elbow deep.

I scoop up handfuls of the one
bug no one seemed to fear as a child.

Was it the rhyme that made us love them?
learning they had children and houses

that would burn? and surely this moment
is the house they flew home to.

Letter to Jim in November

I just finished a poem that
troubled me all summer, a poem

about a man and a tree, and now,
just past Halloween, it has

come together. I just read it and,
of course, thought of sending it

to you, as we've done with our poems
for nearly fifty years. I even

took an envelope out of my desk
but didn't have your address.

Opus vitae

From all the trees that came before it,
the pine learned to whisper, *forever.*

Downrange

When I stepped outside and looked up,
I saw the great, spiraling white
snake of smoke, or vapor, or both,
climbing to where
the booster broke free
and kissed the painful
flare of the rocket on its way
like a fragment
of the sun itself, streaming
east-southeast, fading
in and out and
finally out beyond
the fragile blue air I
was breathing.

And when there was nothing
left to see—in a shift
of senses for a second act—
the earth began trembling
under my feet and
the deep growling
of what I'd just seen
arrived and troubled me
for a minute or
more, troubled me for
an hour past its passing
in the fragile blue air,
still breathing.

Against the Dying of the Light

I was waiting for the evening light
illuminating one brilliant branch high

up in the oak—almost
as a sign—to fade, but it didn't

go, and didn't go, and didn't go,
and didn't go, and

ten minutes later, though night had fallen, I
was still unable to detect any

dimming of the light.

Martha

Our donkey, a deep dredger, calling
up the past every morning, with every

joy and injustice of her life in her song, telling
all of it again and making it new.

Calligraphy

He loved the way a word, seeming suddenly
certain of itself, would appear on the page,

following the strokes of his pen, and
as he watched the sheen of black ink flatten,

would imagine it to be a word he'd
written years before and left

waiting for its yet unknown relatives
to arrive and gather it into a meaning,

without the intention of meaning, maybe
something finally felt he hadn't seen before.

Presence

Something about the brush pile
thirty yards ahead beside the two-
track through the aspen grove,
something too dark, too dense, as
if the glance of a witch
in wait—something out of place.

I whispered the dogs to sit and stay
and held my hand, palm
down, between them to
give my command more weight.

My first thought, always, was of bear. I've
followed the trail of ripped-open
sheepskins, scattered like
piles of bloody popcorn, when
the Basque herders bring
their flocks down from the
mountain pastures
in this late part of summer.

We waited, and the obscure shape
swayed, though not as if in wind.
There was no wind,
only caution becoming fear as
whatever it was rocked
back and forth four times,
building momentum to rise like
a mountain through geologic time, its
murky ridges spreading high against
the pale green of the aspens with
branches of its own, more massive
than these slender trees could take,
and under them,
two black-silver beads, in sunlight blacker

than the darkness they shone out of, sensing
something about our being there.

I felt the dogs quiver, or
maybe it was me.

I wondered how the moose might
see us, three frozen beings pretending
to be small trees or shrubs, pretending
not to breathe, waiting
for him to decide if we were
a threat worth feeling threatened by.

I thought of our neighbor, the blacksmith,
Johnny Reddan, stomped to death
the summer before, out for a short walk
after supper, told his wife
he'd be back before dark.

They found his body the following noon,
a cow with calves, the ranger
said, it must have been a cow. I heard

an airplane sounding angry above
the trees, then it relented to a hard-
edged hum and hummed on
for several minutes, it seemed.

I heard then the kyrie of a red-tailed hawk
and wondered what *she* might be
seeing of our standoff
in this rivery break of ranch road
through the trees. Two

years before a herd of thirteen
moose, five cows and eight
lumbering bulls, spent an idle Christmas
on our snow-covered lawn, rubbing
on the clapboards of the house, nudging

the drift boat on its trailer, locking
antlers, aimlessly pushing each other
around, with no agenda. It seemed
so safe with the solid walls
around us, smiling at
the mangy pelts and
homely mugs, that docile
consciousness at play.

Time was all around us now, meaning
one more siphoned breath of
the air the moose was breathing, too.
I wondered if he could smell us—nothing
moving anywhere.

A fly buzzed by my ear.

Was the bull waiting
for us to break the spell?
His mooseness was implacable,
the light behind him from the trees.

Eight miles south in the town of Driggs,
Deb was at the Safeway for tomatoes,
lettuce, bacon, and bread, expecting
I'd be home for lunch.

The dogs were so still I almost
forgot them, their noses locked
on the moose like
pointers on a grouse.

I scanned the grove for a gap
between two slender trunks,
just wide enough for me.

And then there *was* a breeze.
The grass heads nodded.
A sudden flutter through

the leathery leaves—one breath
was all, as tentative
as our own. It seemed
enough to move the scene.

The bull swayed again
and swung himself one step into the forest
and then another. We heard
dry branches whisper and snap
as he plowed his way,
a primeval wave of midday
darkness through the fragile trees.

The dogs stayed close the last
quarter mile through the aspens
till the track opened out onto a prairie
of scrubby sage and yellow arrowroot.

This Afternoon

I dozed off in my reading chair, and
woke to a view of shelves, the

jumble of books across the room,
and saw Life, all that

examined and reimagined
life and thought,

"How beautiful. How Beautiful," like

oxygen in air.

II

O pitiful lovers of Earth, why are you keeping
Such count of beauty in the ways you wander?
Why are you so insistent on the sweeping

Poetry of sky and sea?

WALLACE STEVENS

Knowledge

The puppy's pinpoint tooth-marks
gracing the cover of this journal,

impressed in it over a decade ago
by the old dog now huffing at

the far end of the couch,
and the three torn pages of

Thich Nhat Hanh teachings she consumed—
Pebble Falling through a Stream,

Yourself, Your Skeleton, and
Emptiness—all she needed,

reminding us we are food, exactly
equal to our hunger.

After Dinner

It was when I stepped out
to take a leak and was noticing

how many branches of the sheltering
oaks were invading the eaves and needed

to be cut back, that the hawk, a falcon
in fact, flashed from the green entanglements

to a roof tile not five feet above
my eye. The air went missing and everything

I might have sensed moving fled
with my breath under the quick

solemn snap-roll glances of this compact
new lord of impending night, honoring me,

I took it that way, my heartbeat

chanting thank you, thank you, thank you, without quite
caring who *you* was.

Palm

The poem *must give pleasure,* Stevens,
with small reason, proclaimed, though

the scale of pleasure ascends into terror, and
the pleasure is in being alive.

It must change, and so it
changes, or is it *I*-the-Perceiver

coming back to the first idea changed,
as a hand changed by its touches?

Thought stirs the basin, and it
fills with flashing silver argentines, each

a sun within a galaxy of water, and when
thought withdraws its hand, the water

clears and is still.

Artichoke

An interminable artichoke, Neruda
called his heart, and isn't *heart*

a synecdoche for *life,* and
does not our life, at times,

seem endlessly enduring?
Until it doesn't.

I may have been the only
kid in my Midwestern town to have

had intimate knowledge of an artichoke,
to have learned the patient pleasure

of peeling away fibrous leaves,
each only a tease for

the taste of the one to follow,
more ritual than meal,

keeping its reward just
out of reach, like foreplay,

each tooth-raked sample,
a little closer to the prize,

till, with a sharp-edged spoon, you
scrape the choke away and reveal

the purely-heart heart of a thistle
you've just destroyed.

Other

When I had yet to learn the nature
of words, I had no sense
the trees and animals
I walked among were something
I was not.

Only when I saw
the swallow fly into the glass
of the window I was
watching through,
and picked it up,
and felt its life struggle
to get back inside,
as its eyes closed
and its head shook
and my hand felt its body
cool and become
a *thing* somewhere
beyond a glass
that wouldn't let me through.

Avalokiteśvara

Standing at almost five feet, the level of my heart
now, I knew you first as Kuan Yin, stone

woman from China I had to look up to see
when I needed to be heard, having no notion

this was precisely who you were, *hearer*
of the cries of the world, you who must have

heard the cries of my life from the very
beginning of my memory, waiting

in the grove of cedars in my grandfather's
garden, behind the house of my earliest

awareness, to hear, without judgment,
my complaints of childhood injustice,

my heartbreak, losing the dog whose fur
I clung to as I took my first steps, dog

who had been my constant companion,
my ever-forgiving, other me, how could she

not *be* anymore when I came home
from school, something no one could explain,

nor coax me to any
comfort, until I began

to hear, in my own words,
cries no longer mine alone.

Against the Whitewashed Palings

I was born the day before the first
air raid on Britain and, of course, remember

nothing of that. But I remember
the things that were spoken about

the war and the way people looked
when they spoke about it. I remember

the German prisoner of war camp in
our little town, only a few blocks

from our house, remember, from the
black-and-white newsreel films, the

Nazi Stuka dive bombers, screaming
through sirens fixed on their wings

to make their deadly terror even
more terrible to those about to die

and to those who remembered the
terrified dying, and the scars, if only

in the memories of those telling it, and
the names from the radio and the

ink-soaked names on the front
pages of the newspapers I picked up

from the sidewalk—El Alamein,
Corregidor, Saipan, Tarawa, Bastogne,

Buchenwald, Guadalcanal, Dresden, Iwo
Jima, the Bulge, Hiroshima, Dunkirk—

remember the young men in khaki
who came to our house to see my sister,

the off-duty guards from the prison camp
who came to drink and play pinochle

with my mother and Martha, my nanny—
my father away in Washington for the war—

the jokes and laughter through
the haze of Camels and Lucky Strikes,

and the blue stars in the windows of
families with fathers, husbands, and sons

away in the war and two of those stars
turning gold for Mrs. Jackson across

the street whose husband's destroyer went down
in the Coral Sea and Mrs. Keller, catty-

corner to our house, whose son Jack
burned up in the sky over Dresden,

the fox holes I dug in the sand at
our cottage where I waited for the Japanese

ships to loom up on the far Lake Michigan
horizon, remember the piercing blue

of the morning glories against the
whitewashed palings out our kitchen

door where I stood when I heard
on the radio of a great bomb

dropped on Japan, and a few days
later, when my mother gave me the

key to open a neighbor's cottage for
two men delivering a mattress and

how the one walking backwards as
he carried the front end of it said,

"Hey kid, did you hear, the war's
over?" and I ran back up the long drive,

the road so much longer and the
gravel deeper, running home to

tell my mom that now everything
would be all right, forever.

Fugitive Blue

Day after timeless summer day, hiding
in the dunes above the big lake,

naked on his belly, from a sandy ridge
watching for the Sheriff of Nottingham,

the Waffen-SS, the Chiricahua
Apaches who would stake him out, a boy

coated with honey in the desert where
the fire ants would eat him alive,

but mostly the Japanese he'd seen
in a magazine photo, preparing

to behead an American sailor
with a samurai sword, across

a big water, on a sandy beach,
like this one, for the war, just ended,

played on in him, alone in those
Sahara-like hollows broken only

by a few sparse clumps
of quack grass, high

above the lake that loomed out
endlessly to the west, like

the Pacific of his nightmares
and his sometime paradise

dreams of brilliance and sand
in which he would become

the sky and watch all
the now-confused pursuers

of his imagined life from the
freedom of his blue disguise.

Radio, 1946

Like windows flashing
from a passing train,
the gibbous moon, now,
and now, and now,
through the peaks of roadside
hemlock and pine, made the boy
almost forget he was even
there, alone in the cavernous
backseat of the Ford convertible,
chasing its headlights through
the warm summer night.

Just ahead, in the light
from the dash, there was
music, there were the
silhouettes of a man
and a woman
who may also have forgotten
he was there behind them,
as if in the steady thump
of tires over tar strips and
the glissading trombone
and clarinet from the radio
he was only the feeling
between them in that moment,
pressed together behind the wheel, only
the rhythm of the moonlight,
of the road and the pulse
of music through the trees,
alone in the speeding island of peace,
held together alone, speeding
through the still,
still summer night.

Corsair

Those childhood summers just
after the war when the planes came back,

a blue Navy Hellcat or gull-winged Corsair, low
and slow and just offshore, almost

eye level from the height of the dunes
often with the cockpit canopy

open, and one time, I swear,
the pilot waved at me, and I flew

on with him a good way down the beach,
watching the surf skimming under

my wings, feeling the throb of that vast
engine as it faded into the still

morning where I listened after
all the sound was gone.

That September

Dead dog, a beagle-looking
dog with a bullet hole, a clean crater

where its right ear had been,
lying on its side, as if asleep

among torn cardboard and rotting oranges,
likely a stray picked up by one of the two

town cops who brought it to the dump
to be with everything else not wanted.

It was just around the hill from the dump
where five hundred German prisoners of

war had dug the village a swimming hole,
probably where my nine-year-old

body picked up polio in late summer
of 1949, just beginning fourth grade.

The polio was terrible and rained
down over my young life for less

than a year, but the dog, the beagle,
as if asleep with the bullet in its ear,

is here right now.

Electric Chair

Specter of my young life, and now
my old life, too, this hallway

of absolute dark. The Rosenbergs
had two sons. The recurring

dream: my mother being dragged
down a corridor of absolute dark

through blinding white circles
of overhead glare

and me pursuing the shadow men
dragging her through the scathing

light they will use to kill her,
the burning circles I cross to

make them give her back, to tell me why
they are killing my mother again.

The Rosenbergs had two sons. Their
mother and father strapped in a

big wooden chair and set on fire, for real,
no hero, no rescue, no happiness, that

the people are killing the only mother
of the two sons and nothing

they can do about it and
nothing I can do.

The Lost House

See each thing in this entire world
as a moment of time.
DŌGEN, 1233

The one sobering apparition
that had greeted our return each June,

half a mile up the beach—we
were never quite sure how far—

half-collapsed and clinging
to a cliff in the shadows

of three enshrouding pines
whose roots seemed all that held

the surviving structure in place after
the sand dune on which it sat

surrendered to years of pounding storms and
the rising level of Lake Michigan.

The brown of the shakes and
the interior shadows had further

darkened with soaking and rot
in the gloom of the pines,

with several limbs grown
through spaces where windows

looked out, no longer
a structure separate from the trees.

It would have been easy to imagine
the house as a shipwreck pitched

up on the cliff in a horrendous storm
or as a morbid dollhouse, cut away

to expose the life inside, or
where the life had been, and

there *was* life: cliff swallows
that fashioned gourd-like

nests along the eaves and
the yellow mud-dauber wasps that

stung like "tarnation," we were told,
and once I saw a fox with three

kits close by and wondered if she
had her den in there, wondered

about the people who seemed to have
simply fled the wreckage that had been

their aerie on the vastness of the lake
with the silhouettes of ore boats

and freighters, backlit Xanadu's
taking forever across the horizon.

꙳

There were dares to climb up into the cave
of the derelict house and the story

of a boy who died in there,
in a very strange way, bled out

from a wound just right of his right eye,
having hurled rocks and loosened bricks

at crumbling wallboard until
one missile bounced back, they figured,

into his temple, though no one
I knew remembered his name.

꙳

And summers later, we returned
to find the haunted wreckage gone,

the receding cliff all bare white sand,
with a few clumps of couch grass

and in the lapping of the lake on the beach
below, the amphibious body of one ancient pine.

Between storms the great lake rises
and falls, unnoticed, like breath

if you aren't paying attention,
as the clock continues, whether or not you

think of time. The silent ships
passing. On calm days you might believe,

with only a little determination
you could walk out to one of those

ships and be one of the deckhands
leaning on the taffrail, gazing back

at the distant shore. All the summers
we told our friends the legends of the house,

the little we knew and the more we heard
from year to year, and then the summer

we couldn't be quite sure where
the house had ever been.

Special Attention

for Guy de la Valdène

He remembered being mugged thirty years before
on a fair winter's morning near Bangkok.

He'd taken a longboat up the Chao Phraya,
stopped at the floating market to

buy a bunch of bananas the size of a
small Christmas tree, and when the

boatman wanted to put in at a stream-
side settlement to buy rice,

walked into the one small shop
to look at the curios a tourist might

look at, and then, stepping
back out onto a porch, had been

grabbed, pulled around the corner,
pushed up against the wall and

patted down as if asked, at preflight security,
to step aside for special attention,

which he was just then receiving from the
trunk of a baby elephant about the

size of a Volkswagen bus,
for the bananas she could smell on

his clothes, how she held his arm
with her trunk while she walked him

back to the boat, and one by one,
skins and all, took each yellow fruit

to her mouth and fired it down her throat so
eagerly he could hear it tunk in her

gullet, and with the bunch stripped
to a bare stem, lay her fire-hose trunk

on his shoulder and seemed to give
him a gentle squeeze before

swinging her head toward the curio
shop and following it back to work.

Navajo

The rug I'm sitting on reveals
a secret of which its

weaver may no longer be aware:
the way the shuttle moved so swiftly

through the conscious forest of
the warp her hands so lovingly prepared.

Tourist, 1963

He wandered the streets of Madrid
in October, imagining the

Guadarramas he could catch a glimpse of
to the northwest from a few high

places in the city and would drive to
a few days after the Prado and

flamenco singers piercing him with the
pain of their singing and sizzling

bowls of baby eels, thin as spaghetti,
sautéed in oil, garlic, and peppers and

a bullfight with a rejoneador
stabbing a bull from horseback till

the banderillas hung like a
thicket of storm-wasted bamboo from

the bull's bleeding shoulders and trying
to talk with Spaniards, in bars, about

Franco and having them look at him as
if he'd told them he'd just farted and

expected them to find that interesting,
imagining himself as Robert Jordan who

would drive up into the mountains past
La Granja to study a bridge that

needed to be blown up for noble reasons, if
he knew anything about dynamite and

structural geometry, and
a girl with a tragic history he would

fall in love with before, unlike
Robert Jordan, driving to Segovia for

a sumptuous lunch under an aqueduct and a day
later to Toledo to discover the tiny furniture

in the house of El Greco.

February 25, 1970

The scrim of the sky almost
radiating blue—a rare,

midwinter break in the clouds and
lake-effect snow that would keep us

longing for light from November
into spring—the day,

still, sharp, and clear, with
a little actual warmth from the

sun you could feel when you
turned your face up to it—a day

fragile and dazzling, above
the still-crystalline snow, and

in the evening, savoring the last of it
as I drove out toward the county

road, hearing the news
on public radio that

Mark Rothko—whose grave
canvases had not yet

taken possession of me—was dead, and,
remembering it now as a premonition

of something I would come to love,

how the deep azure of the sky to the east
and the darkening white plane of

the pasture below it dwelt there, just about equally.

Ahead of All Parting

for Carl Rakosi

Night after night, the dreams of his hand,
the pistol barrel turning his way, the
cylinder revolving one click as the
hammer retracts, the scene set, and
the bullet nosing out of the muzzle.

Night sweats and the declaration:
No, not this, No. Not *this* kind of No.

Scenes from a movie you fast-forward through.

The old poet listened and then
told him the custom
where a young man must tell
the shaman of his dreams
and of one youth who told of being chased
by a bear and, in the frenzy
of his flight, running off the lip
of a high canyon wall,
waking in terror of gravity.

Next time, hit the bottom,
the shaman had said.

Next time—the old poet told him—
let the dream-bullet blow your fear away.

Earth Angel

Mark Rothko, *Untitled* (*Black on Gray*),
1969

One of his last canvases—actually
black and medium earth-brown—

has come to live in me. "The dark
is always at the top," he said,

as before me now, on the mind's altar,
the scary, infinite, and finally

comforting black space above
the warm brown plane of earth,

stretching out to meet
the dark in which we stand.

But in the earth-realm, down
and just off to the left, a chorus

of under-painting swirls to send
my eye *a necessary angel,*

from a column of the dust it raised.

Being Tree

What we care for, we will grow to resemble.
And what we resemble will hold us, when
we are us no longer....
RICHARD POWERS

From Ovid, he knew this
happened more than once

before, as reward for a compassionate life,
refuge from the immolating lust of a god,

or just sitting long enough under a tree
to forget doing—feeling, seeing, sensing

from the hearts of sightless Things, living
more intensely than ever intended

for eyes, and thought how brave it would be
to stand witness over the light on the hills

out of which he grew, to be a shepherd
of shadows, lingering, moving with clouds

over rocks and steep meadows, giving
voice to the day-shaping wind in all

its intonations, to hold the earth together,
taking life and stories from centuries of soil

with roots of neighboring trees entwined
inextricably with his own, bringing

sugary tannins to his brooding limbs and leaf-
bearing fingers, transforming sunlight into

the breathable color of air.

Correspondence

Like dwindling echoes gathered far away
Into a deep and thronging unison
BAUDELAIRE

He remembered how late afternoon sunlight
reflected off the water, upslope through

lakeside ferns and the intricate weaving
of boughs, onto the ceiling of what had been

their bedroom then, and how, with a breeze
crazing the water a little as he watched, the

brilliance around and between the shadows
of beech leaves and feathers of hemlock

brought a kind of trance-like fascination,
when he gave himself up to it, and remembered

this through the pentatonic clanging
of the wind chimes thrashing in the blue oak just

outside the window where he sat now, three
thousand miles and forty years away.

III

What I have not done was therefore perfectly beautiful,
in perfect keeping with the impossibility of being done.

PAUL VALÉRY

Uncertainty

Always the fear, not of death
itself, the dying or the being dead,

but the uncertainty of what
may happen on the way, which

is a fear of the living
we must do, of getting lost

in pain, or forgetfulness,
of not being ourselves

right up to the end
of something only

our fleeting selves
have ever really feared?

Valéry

So is there no "world" touching this one
inside the mind?

Only on Earth, where all our
ideas of life come together,
observing our endless episodes of terror

and the fruitful accommodations we evolve,
creating a god from the inversion
of our imperfections, you took note,

the dark to our light, according both
to the weather and to our moods,
which the god would have also, and

if *she* exists here, would we not
know her, as subject knows shadow
wherever there is light?

After Daphne

Watching the last horizon-
hugging light of Venus, magnified

through a bower of the leaves
of two coastal live oaks

a hundred feet more distant
from where I stand in a light

wind, something Venus doesn't know,
streaming through this foliage

so ineluctably bestowed by
a mind inclined to see her this way.

Becoming a Tree

Little by little I am becoming a tree.
No, my feet not reaching deep

into the long-buried past to find
food, nor is my skin thickening

to cambium to protect my
soft being from bugs, worms, and

weather, my fingers are not becoming
spindly, budding *chloroplastid* leaves,

nor my shadow casting more shadows
over half the backyard, but

if a spotted towhee were to
perch on my shoulder a moment, I

wouldn't mind, or not mind.

Saying Goodbye to the Pines

The once dark needles
flair a fiery bronze in
the day's early light and splay
like cross-hatching over the drive
after last night's sundowner wind.

Something I didn't think would happen
before the last day of my life,
but now it seems that I may live on
in an almost pineless world.

Five years of drought and ever-
accruing heat have been more than
they can bear.

Tomorrow Humberto Tapia
will come to take these four towering
wind-ciphers down,
leaving only rank air
in the wake of his saws.

Their whisper of *peace* in the
afternoon breeze
will have to find its voice
in *our* breathing now, the way,
even sometimes this far inland, we
sense the slow-breaking voice of the sea.

Stealth

Deer come close in the late afternoon,
at ease on the dry grass under

the oaks around the house in what
they sense to be a coyote-free zone,

a mountain-lion-safe space, enjoying
the shaded heat, as I am, this doe,

an easy stone's throw away
from one who has eaten her kind.

I employ all my stealth, slipping
my hand slowly over the rough

cotton of my shirt to reach my note-
book and pen, taking her life down

in this moment, as quiet as I can.

Moon, Again

I watched the moon taking the
measure of the sun again and

told her not to bother: it's
all just shadow play, I said.

She didn't smile or frown, she
just continued gazing down

with the coolness of affection
your mother once had, saying

I told you so, with-
out saying anything at all.

A Monk's Life

Richard Brautigan, 1935–1984

In the breaks from monasteries,
dokusans, tea and silence, I

would hang out with Brautigan in
Tokyo where his royalties

paid for a tall suite at the top
of a tall hotel, everything

about him was tall, as when
we walked in Shinjuku,

eyes grew wide at the
approach of his long blond

mustache and black stovepipe
cowboy hat, making him

so tall he was famous, as
translated in Japan.

Distant Rain

I cannot keep the pear blossoms from withering,
Li Ch'ing-chao wrote a thousand years ago; still

I watch them closely, loving each gathering
wrinkle as it rises, like the creased

flesh on the back of my still *warm*
and capable hand.

On Dyslexia

Words on the page and the com-
positions of geometry tend

toward entropy. You
see them as they are; I

see them as they are
becoming.

Haunted

And how bewildered is any womb-born
creature that has to fly.
RAINER MARIA RILKE

The bats who hang in the dark, chittering
from our eaves, seem
members of our house we haven't
yet had time to name. We feel them
in the night air around us and catch
a glimpse of the movement
of their wings in the half-light of the moon.
Mouse-angels, terrifying and warm, mythical,
seeming almost terrified themselves,
skittering after the echoes of
their own voices homing in
on the smaller creatures of the night
and also on larger, winged beings hunting
their bat-blood to stay alive.

And this morning I found one of them asleep,
hanging from the inside of a window screen
in our still half-darkened bedroom, and
wondered how it had gotten in and
why it wasn't sleeping with the other
members of its choir, if it had been
expelled or simply gotten lost?
I covered it with a child's
plastic drinking cup and slid a large
jack of diamonds playing card under
the lip while I carried it out to the yard.

The bat landed on its back, spreading
the intricate framework of its wings
to right itself while I waited
to see if it could fly, as I remembered reading

that rabid bats can't, and that my friend Ted,
having been bitten trying to help a fallen bat,
had needed a battery of painful injections
to sear the rabies away.

The bat struggled up on its pinions,
dragging itself through the grass as if
trying to reach me for help,
but I, fearing rabies, and for our dogs,
killed it with a shovel, not then knowing
that a bat can't take flight from the ground,
must have a perch to receive the grace
of air under its wings. I could have
released it in the crotch of a tree, on
a window ledge . . .

I picked up the skin of a ripped balloon
on the tip of the shovel and
carried it to the trash, protecting
our house and this faltering world
from what may have been just
the physics of being a bat. Maybe
the world won't miss one bat. Maybe
I did the right thing. But the world, my world,
is missing it, crawling toward me for life.

Almost Dying

*When one has had the psychological
experience of this state,
One knows the serenity that comes
before death.*
TAISEN DESHIMARU

The deep-down feeling I will
live forever, what-

ever *I* might mean—
amazed how fast

this fleeting identity
had served its time,

"Oh, that's too bad," I
thought, seeing its long-loved

life trailing off
into this last moment, though

last of what? I
didn't seem to care.

"Love Is Everything"

Snow drifting in the windless dark,
a million dusky parachutes

floating down on k.d. lang, who is standing
barefoot on the stage of the Santa

Barbara Bowl, singing "Love Is Everything,"
and we are loving it up in the

cheap seats where we could see the Pacific
until it got dark, flakes falling on us, too,

up here, in our wild surmise, the meltless
snow of ash from the great fire

consuming the mountains above us
for sixty days and nights, and

now a silent dirge of ash raining
on us all, the cremated remains

of trees, deer, grasshoppers,
rattlesnakes, and doves, sucked up into

a billowing crown of midafternoon
heat, now cooling in darkness

to the point of letting go, this
enchanting translation of terror.

Out of the Blue

A cluster of bright white thistle feathers
drifts by, an octave above the stream,

free-range Pleiades on the
lam from last night's sky.

Kilimanjaro

Once, in sight of Kilimanjaro,
I stopped for a young Maasai

crouched by the road, blood
glistening from his nose and

oozing from the gash across his ribs.
"Get in," I said in Swahili.

"What happened?" I asked.
"Mbuni," he said.

"Ostrich?" I said in English.
"Yes! Ostrich!" he replied.

"They tend to be wild."

Below the Laurel Tree

A poem found in the table of contents
of Willis Barnstone's *Border of a Dream:
Selected Poems of Antonio Machado*

The torn cloud, the rainbow, and he was
the demon of my dream, from the doorsill

of a dream, those children in a row, stained
by earlier days, the house I loved before

the pale canvas of the afternoon, tranquil
afternoon, almost, like Anakreon, O luminous

afternoon! It is an ashen and shabby evening.
Will the spellbound world die with you? Naked

is the earth. Field to an old distinguished
gentleman. Yesterday my sorrows, perhaps

the hand in dreaming. You will know
yourself below the laurel tree.

Late

Death grows a little more in me each day

history slight as an offstage whisper

getting it almost right again   almost

a month disappears on this page

watching out the window *this world that is ours*

and the profusion of birds flying by.

The Ecstasies of Sense

If there's any former life inside
this almost transparent, honey-

colored cube of amber, it's
too small to see, except for a

few tiny bubbles of ancient air, even
through a 10× loupe, just

the gold clarity that, looking,
brings a sweetness to the

buds of my tongue and the
glands of my cheeks,

to make them want the
taste of this parallax clarity,

warmed to the color of the
nothing I see.

Mid-April near Santa Ynez

Sunlight, after last night's rain,
breaking clouds apart, light

snow sifted through Coulter pines
on the highest slopes,

dust-screen of yesterday's desert
wind washed back down

into the sage—
sky scrubbed clean—

air incandescent—
all the way to the sea.

The Distaff Tarantula

Weaves her diaphanous
flag—pearly with dew—
on the new spring green of the hillside.

"Come on down for a real good time,"
her silver sign says. "You
won't live to regret it."

Flit

The afternoon cast pewter as
the clouds edge in, a dome

of baric stillness waiting
for some thing, any thing,

the flit of a single wing as
a tin-gray titmouse drops from

a low-hanging branch for seed.

Us

The color of air is in our eyes,
the colors of everything visible, our

voices making syllables of
the wind that gets inside us,

speaking through the space we breathe
in praise of the air, whose creatures we affirm

ourselves, with every inhalation.

And, just now, a hummingbird.

IV

So, even nature, trying,
From age to age, from face to other face,
To reach the best of beauty in your eyes,
Must now be old, like me, and close to death.
That is why terror, mixed with beauty, feeds
So strangely my desire:
I cannot think, or tell, what hurts or helps
Me more, after I gaze upon your face, —
The end of nature or this happiness.

MICHELANGELO

(translated by Joseph Tusiani,
from poems to Vittoria Colonna)

Landscape at Eighty

A lifetime burning in every moment, Eliot
wrote of his life in old age, but

when does *old age* begin? do we know? We
seem to agree on the ending.

The blue reaches of a summer afternoon.
A turkey vulture tilting on its wings.

A crow finishes its drink and flaps
off, like old leather, to an oak.

When I look up again, the hawk, hovering in winds aloft,
has faded into the sky,

and the lizard hasn't budged from the rock since
I first spotted him there.

We're always watched by familiar eyes, the
countless windows in which we appear,

the spider on the pillow taking in all
eight of me at a glance.

Beauty still lies in wait, whispering under all the noise—
lurking in ambush behind a distraction,

seducing with a breeze, scent of spruce,
gardenia, subtle rose,

warm fragrance of sleeping dog, a
whistle off the end of each snore.

Luminous blue rivers shuttle through the Greenland glacier,
never swift enough to suit themselves.

Bananas passing from green to brown,
barely pausing at yellow.

Poet: a worm whose words might
make a butterfly.

Li Po drowned embracing the moon of illusion
in the river, reflecting the moon

of illusion in the sky, loving both equally, but
the moon in the river was closer.

Nepenthe will keep you from weeping.
I carry my claws with care.

Coruscating light all day on the river—
all night on the walls of my room.

I find myself nostalgic for the
last time I was feeling nostalgic.

I used to be there all the time,
looking back on it now.

All night, the quiet night of California,
freeways full or filling up.

One certain liberty—
to be patient and, eventually, leave.

I ward off death reviving drowned bees
and carrying errant spiders out of the house.

Cirrus clouds stacked up for beauty,
nothing else to account for it.

This joy needs no reason to reach me.

Cézanne subjected himself to the landscape every day
and drew his religion from it.

The horse sees the two nearly identical
worlds in which we live.

My late afternoon shadow,
fifteen feet tall.

Do you fear the world will die
and leave you behind?

A landscape is the abstract, of every
hill, shadow, and mystery it comprises

in the self-forgetful moment of a
mind not striving to define it.

The landscape is a complex being; its
survival may depend on our demise—

more urgently watching what Earth
is doing with its atmosphere, *things we've never*

seen before, becoming a cliché, the news,
a daily booster shot of *leaden-eyed despair.*

Sometimes the only green left in the tree is
the mistletoe that siphoned it off.

Hatred of Knowledge has a life all its own, as
anything addicted to extinction must.

Time wouldn't miss a tick if we were gone.
And who would there be to remember?

Without poetry the visible and invisible
worlds wouldn't be aware of each other, would

obscure the mind's invention of knowledge
between a cloud of dust and a cinder.

Three deer on the hilltop, their
ears keeping watch while they doze.

The high step of the blind dog
testing the air he walks into.

Waxing moon, swelling each night,
gobbling a hundred more stars.

The poppy flourishes to beguile the bee and, by
its nature, catches me.

Hummingbird buzzing a foot from my face,
wondering if I contain nectar?

When I realize I'm dreaming, I
know I'm not asleep.

How words you courted half your life
arrive on their own one summer night when

you're doing nothing with all your might.
Poetry is the part you can't explain.

We won't blame ourselves for making so much
of a little construction of words.

Sanity is waiting here outside your door.
It might be raining sanity, or

blowing sanity, or the
sanity of silence with just a few birds.

Pärt said his music, like white light, contains all the colors and
only the prism of a listener can make them appear.

How many times have you tried
to explain the earth to a worm?

Sphere: energy and gravity in divine embrace.

When the *I who am not I* meets
the you who never arrived.

Ryōkan, on the secret of his art: *one
two three four five six seven.*

Counting to a billion will take you thirty-four years, if
you don't lose your concentration.

These Things are empty, and when
you become empty, they become luminous.

No one who has seen a quark has ever forgotten it.

I spent years waiting for patience and
found it in no time at all.

"I don't believe in last meals," Jim said,
"I believe in lots of last meals."

Nights we sat out under the stars
while the lights in the hills blinked out.

Pole: place from which anywhere you step will
be in the right direction.

When we die we'll be what we've always been, an
urn of dust on loan from the stars.

My breath would keep a lion alive.
My blood would nourish an eagle.

Ages ago, I surrendered to nature so this
page could be here and not be blank.

Wishing I could introduce my grandson to my father.

And God so loved the world he gave himself up
and became the world.

Then Knowledge Is the Only Life

Faustus suffered not because he bargained away
his soul to possess all knowledge but

because the bargain left him with no
new life to breathe, nothing left to learn.

You can't see far into reflecting
water, and with a breeze, it's

thousand-moon-lake dazzling
and glares you down into your

other senses, the perfume of music, the haunting
silence of bees,

the boat's gentle rocking in the
field of stars you're rowing on.

That Particular Poem

Detonated an old truth, gnawing
a long time at the edge of his mind, that

he had loved her more than she
was able to love him, a fact

as natural as the color of leaves,
that one of two must always love more, that

one must always love more.

Along the Uaso Nyiro

I once sat six feet from a lion on
a long, hot afternoon along the

Uaso Nyiro, just south of Somalia,
an old, red-maned lion, a dozen

scars around his eyes, his mane
skewed and drooping (as if

tired of making him look fierce),
chewed-up and dethroned,

tolerated by his pride, an outlier
now, following for scraps, though

he kept his dignity while I
mused with him, as if we'd been

friends somewhere once before,
close enough to hear his

sad breathing
through the open window of the truck.

My trust in his lionness kept me from
reaching out to scratch his ragged ears,

but that was five lion-
generations ago, thinking of it

now, from the banks of no river,
an outlier nursing his pride of

late friends, a short
while from nothing at all.

Tending the Moon in My Barn

> *Your mind is the kingdom,*
> *Your nature, the king.*
> HUI NENG

Names are falling away from their Things,
like leaves grown tired of a tree.

Sometimes I lose them for a second, some-
times long enough to make me

laugh at my memory, a naked uncle still
proud of his now only half-remembered socks.

I see everything as I walk toward it, or past it, or
into the sparse grass I imagine just ahead.

The Best Part

Never more happiness, never
a greener stillness of the leaves

than the blue-gray darkness
of the summer afternoon, alone

in the house of his childhood,
the dense air heavy on the

heavy trees around the house,
its walls and windows pressing

the gathering storm around
the jubilant child who isn't there.

Collected Works

As if he held another
body in his hands

and turned it over
and looked at it

and wondered where
to set it down.

Barn burned down—now I can see the moon
Mizuta Masahide
(1657–1723)

The Poem I Haven't Written about the Moon in My Barn

Wishing

To depart as air, for what is
left of my earthly being to

be purified by the turkey vulture
or even that magnifico,

the condor, grotesque at rest yet
sublime in flight, that I may be

consumed by the soaring birds
that have carried me

so high above the valley,
becoming invisible, in

and out of the blue, to
anyone still watching.

Stay

What do you see? I asked my dog as we
stopped a moment, both of us trans-

fixed by a sudden gust of wind, and she
wanted to watch and listen and to smell

the world we were discovering a little
longer, and though I tried to urge her

back toward home, I
was happy she made me stay.

Rue, not rage
Against that night
We go into,
Sets me straight
On what to do
Before I die—
Sit in the shade,
Look at the sky

SAMUEL MENASHE

About the Author

Dan Gerber is the author of nine previous volumes of poetry, most recently *Particles: New and Selected Poems* (Copper Canyon), as well as three novels, a collection of short stories, and two books of nonfiction. His honors include *Foreword* magazine's Gold Medal Book of the Year Award in Poetry, the Society of Midland Authors Award, the Mark Twain Award, and the Michigan Author Award. His poems have appeared in *Poetry, The New Yorker, The Nation, Caliban, The Sun,* and *Best American Poetry.* He and his wife, Debbie, live with their beloved menagerie—domestic and wild—in the mountains of California's central coast.

Poetry is vital to language and living. Since 1972, Copper Canyon Press has published extraordinary poetry from around the world to engage the imaginations and intellects of readers, writers, booksellers, librarians, teachers, students, and donors.

COPPER CANYON PRESS WISHES TO EXTEND A SPECIAL THANKS TO THE FOLLOW-
ING SUPPORTERS WHO PROVIDED FUNDING DURING THE COVID-19 PANDEMIC:

4Culture
Academy of American Poets (Literary Relief Fund)
City of Seattle Office of Arts & Culture
Community of Literary Magazines and Presses (Literary Relief Fund)
Economic Development Council of Jefferson County
National Book Foundation (Literary Relief Fund)
Poetry Foundation
U.S. Department of the Treasury Payroll Protection Program

WE ARE GRATEFUL FOR THE MAJOR SUPPORT PROVIDED BY:

TO LEARN MORE ABOUT UNDERWRITING
COPPER CANYON PRESS TITLES,
PLEASE CALL 360-385-4925 EXT. 103

WE ARE GRATEFUL FOR THE MAJOR SUPPORT PROVIDED BY:

Richard Andrews

Anonymous (3)

Jill Baker and Jeffrey Bishop

Anne and Geoffrey Barker

In honor of Ida Bauer, Betsy
Gifford, and Beverly Sachar

Donna Bellew

Matthew Bellew

Sarah Bird

Will Blythe

John Branch

Diana Broze

John R. Cahill

Sarah Cavanaugh

Stephanie Ellis-Smith and
Douglas Smith

Austin Evans

Saramel Evans

Mimi Gardner Gates

Gull Industries Inc. on behalf of
William True

The Trust of Warren A. Gummow

William R. Hearst III

Carolyn and Robert Hedin

David and Jane Hibbard

Bruce Kahn

Phil Kovacevich and Eric Wechsler

Lakeside Industries Inc. on behalf
of Jeanne Marie Lee

Maureen Lee and Mark Busto

Peter Lewis and Johnna Turiano

Ellie Mathews and Carl Youngmann
as The North Press

Larry Mawby and Lois Bahle

Hank and Liesel Meijer

Jack Nicholson

Gregg Orr

Petunia Charitable Fund and
adviser Elizabeth Hebert

Suzanne Rapp and Mark Hamilton

Adam and Lynn Rauch

Emily and Dan Raymond

Joseph C. Roberts

Jill and Bill Ruckelshaus

Cynthia Sears

Kim and Jeff Seely

Joan F. Woods

Barbara and Charles Wright

In honor of C.D. Wright,
from Forrest Gander

Caleb Young as C. Young Creative

The dedicated interns and
faithful volunteers of
Copper Canyon Press

The Chinese character for poetry is made up
of two parts: "word" and "temple."
It also serves as pressmark for
Copper Canyon Press.

This book is set in PSFournier Pro Light.
Book design by Gopa & Ted2, Inc.
Printed on archival-quality paper.